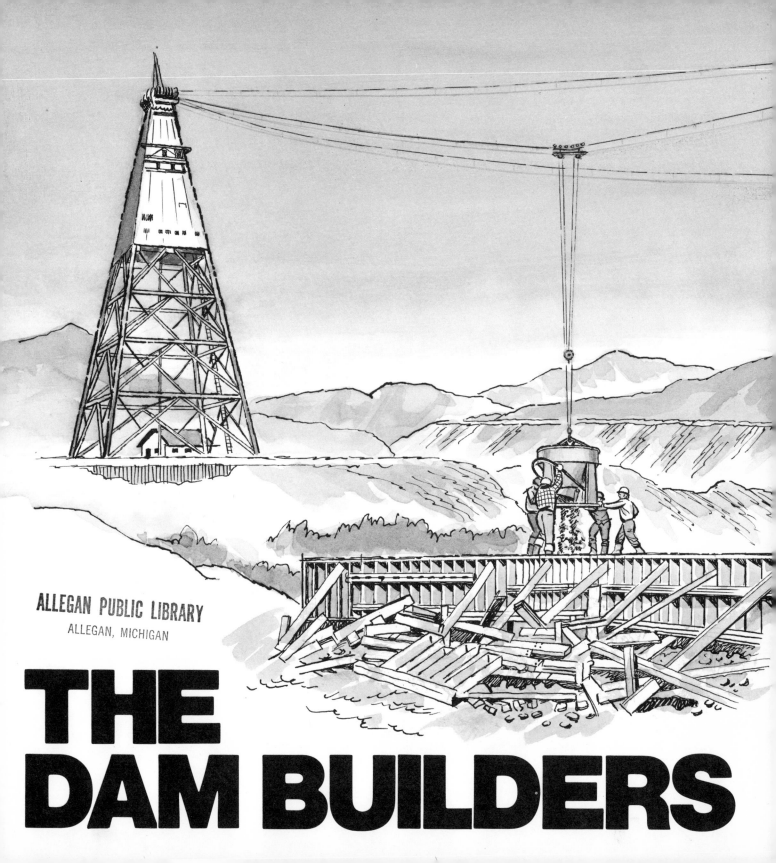

THE DAM BUILDERS

THE DAM

BY
JAMES E. KELLY
AND
WILLIAM R. PARK

DRAWINGS BY
HERBERT E. LAKE

▲ADDISON-WESLEY

BUILDERS

Addisonian Press Titles
by James E. Kelly and William R. Park
THE AIRPORT BUILDERS
THE ROADBUILDERS
THE TUNNEL BUILDERS
THE DAM BUILDERS

 An Addisonian Press Book

Text Copyright © 1977 by James E. Kelly and William R. Park
Illustrations Copyright © 1977 by Herbert E. Lake
All Rights Reserved
Addison-Wesley Publishing Company, Inc.
Reading, Massachusetts 01867
Printed in the United States of America

BCDEFGHIJK-WZ-79

Library of Congress Cataloging in Publication Data
Kelly, James E
  The dam builders.
  "An Addisonian Press book."
  SUMMARY: Traces each step in the design and construction
of earthfill and masonry dams and describes the equipment
and machinery used.
  1. Dams—Juvenile literature. [1. Dams]
I. Park, William R., joint author.
II. Lake, Herbert E., illustrator.
III. Title.
TC540.K44   627'.8   77-5406
ISBN 0-201-05727-1

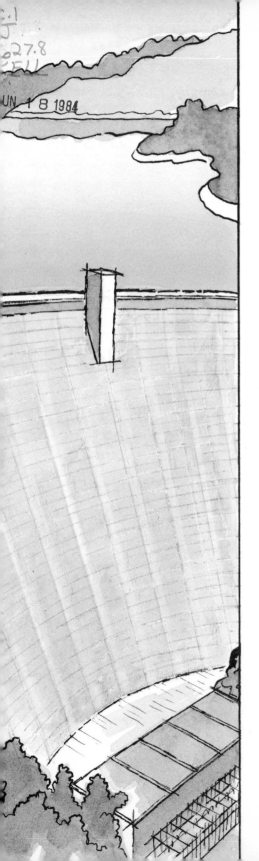

WHY DAMS ARE BUILT

Have you ever seen a big dam or the lake that it forms? If you have, you probably wondered how the dam was built and how it works.

There are many kinds of dams and just as many reasons for building them. Maybe you already know about dams that form the beautiful lakes where people fish and swim and ride in boats. But did you know that dams are also built to prevent floods, to make electricity and to store water so people can use it?

PLANNING A DAM

Much work must be done before a dam can be built.

Many things must be decided.

Where is the best place to build the dam? What kind of dam should it be? Only after these questions are answered, can the plans be prepared.

Civil engineers design the dams and prepare the plans.

The plans show where everything must go and how the dam will be built.

Core drills bring up earth samples for examination.

Civil engineers design and prepare plans.

Contractors must have plans that show how and where everything will go.

Helicopters are sometimes used to measure distances and photograph terrain.

Men using transits will measure hills and valleys.

The engineers use *transits* to measure the hills and valleys. They need to know how high the dam must be built. They need to know how much land will be covered by water when the dam is completed.

The area that drains water into the place where the dam will be built is called the *watershed*. The engineers must figure out how much rain will fall there, then they can decide what kind of dam to build.

Watershed must be mapped.

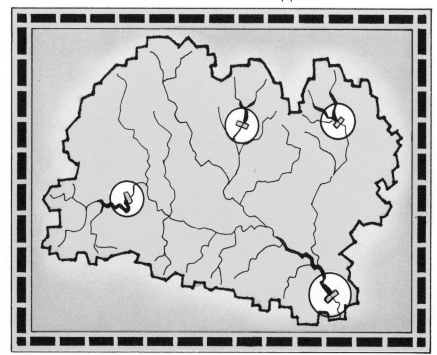

CLEARING THE LAND

Next, the land that will be covered by water must be cleared. All houses and other buildings will be torn down or moved away. Most trees will also be removed.

Small buildings are pushed down by tractors with big steel buckets on the front. These machines are called *tractor-loaders*.

Crawler-loader with logging attachment.

Clearing the land with a tractor wheel loader.

Something must be done to keep the water away from the dam while it is being built. A *diversion ditch* is dug to carry the water around the site.

This ditch is dug with a *crane and dragline.* The crane looks like a machine with a fishing pole. Instead of a fish on the end, a big steel basket is attached to the end of the line. This is called a dragline. One side of the basket is open with sharp steel teeth on the bottom edge. The basket is swung out and dropped on the ground. As it is dragged back toward the crane, the teeth cut into the ground. The basket is filled with dirt. Then the crane swings the basket around and dumps the dirt on the bank.

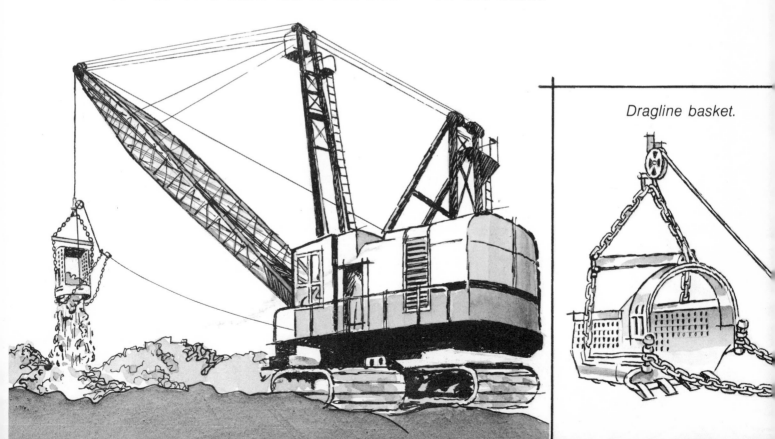

Dragline basket.

EARTHFILL DAMS

Many dams are made mostly of dirt. They are called *earthfill dams*.

It is more than just a big pile of plain dirt. The center of the dam, called the *core*, is made of clay so the water cannot seep through.

Profile or side view of dam.

Roadway across top of dam.

Water.

Core is made of selected clay and watertight material.

Downstream face-grass covered.

Upstream face is lined with riprap.

Ground level.

Core trench.

Drain.

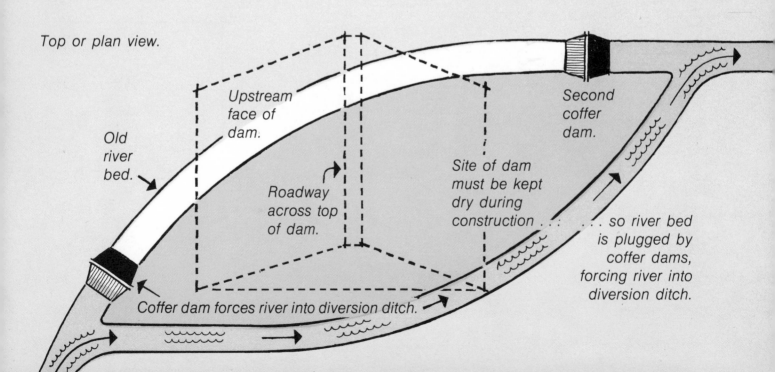

Top or plan view.

Old river bed.

Upstream face of dam.

Roadway across top of dam.

Site of dam must be kept dry during construction . . .

Second coffer dam.

. . . so river bed is plugged by coffer dams, forcing river into diversion ditch.

Coffer dam forces river into diversion ditch.

THE COFFER DAM

When the diversion ditch is completed, a small dam called a *coffer dam* is built to stop the water from going down the old river bed. Instead the water will run down the diversion ditch.

A second coffer dam is built in the river bed below the dam site. This keeps the water that is running out of the downstream end of the diversion ditch from running back into the dam site.

The coffer dam is made by piling dirt and rock across the river bed. It is as high as the top of the diversion ditch so the water will not run over it.

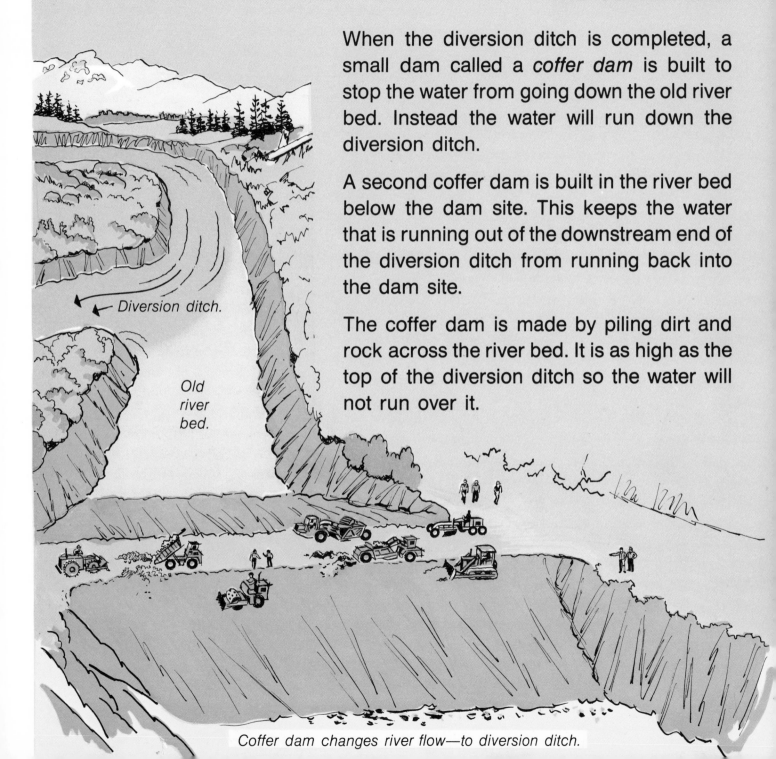

← Diversion ditch.

Old river bed.

Coffer dam changes river flow—to diversion ditch.

MOTOR SCRAPERS

STANDARD SCRAPER.

ELEVATING SCRAPER.

The dirt for the coffer dam is brought by *motor scrapers.* These big machines roll back and forth dumping big loads of dirt on the coffer dam. The front part of the motor scraper is a tractor. The tractor pulls a big scoop behind it. The scoop has wheels on it and it looks like a wagon. A sharp blade on the front of the scoop is lowered against the ground. The tractor grunts and roars as it pulls the wagon along. The blade scrapes the dirt up into the bowl.

When the motor scraper is in the right place to unload, the back wall of the scoop moves forward and pushes the dirt out.

◀ *Apron open.*

When it is time to unload, back wall of scoop moves forward and pushes the dirt out.

CRAWLER LOADER.

CRAWLER DOZER.

CRAWLER TRACTORS AND BULLDOZERS

Scrapers load dirt at the borrow pit.

The place where the scrapers load the dirt is called the *borrow pit.*

Sometimes another kind of tractor is used to push the scrapers and help them load. It is a *crawler tractor* and moves along on steel tracks instead of rubber tires. It is not as fast as the scrapers but it is more powerful.

When a big steel blade is put on the front of a crawler tractor it is called a *bulldozer.* You will see many bulldozers at work pushing big piles of dirt around.

Large twin engine scraper.

Bulldozers push the scrapers and help them to load.

MOTOR GRADERS

MOTOR GRADER.

LARGE 3-AXLE SCRAPER.

The scrapers run back and forth from the dam to the borrow-pit on a *haul road*. A machine called a *motor grader* is used to make the haul road smooth. The motor grader has rubber tires and a big steel blade underneath. The blade scrapes the ground smooth.

A water truck sprays water on the haul road to keep it from getting too dusty.

Scraper and water truck on haul road.

CRANE.   BOTTOM DUMP WAGONS.

BOTTOM DUMPS

The core of the dam must go deep in the ground so that the water cannot seep under it. A *core trench* is dug first.

A dragline scoops up the dirt and drops it into steel wagons that are pulled by rubber-tired tractors. The wagons have doors in the bottom which are opened to let the dirt out. The wagons are called *bottom dumps*.

Digging core trench with dragline.

FRONT-END LOADERS

FRONT-END WHEEL LOADERS.

CRAWLER LOADER.

When the core trench is finished, it is ready to be filled. The bottom dumps are loaded with clay by *front-end loaders.*

The huge rubber tires on the front-end loaders are so big that you could just barely roll them through the door of a house.

A large steel scoop on the front of the machine moves up and down. It lifts the clay up and dumps it into the bottom dump.

COMPACTORS

PNEUMATIC ROLLER.   SHEEPSFOOT COMPACTOR.   VIBRATORY COMPACTOR.

The clay in the core must be packed down so that it will be watertight.

Compactors roll back and forth across the dirt as it is unloaded from the bottom dumps. The compactors have big steel drums that roll along like wheels. The drums have steel knobs or pads sticking out on them. The knobs push into the ground and pack it down until it is hard.

A water truck sprays water on the dam, making it easier to compact.

BUILDING UP THE EARTHFILL DAM

LARGE-FOOT COMPACTOR.   OFF-HIGHWAY TRUCK.

As the watertight core rises above the ground, regular dirt is dumped on each side of it. This dirt is also packed down by compactors. The dirt on the side of the dam where the water comes from is called the *upstream shell.* The dirt on the other side is called the *downstream shell.*

The downstream shell is built with a layer of sand at the bottom. This layer of sand runs up the side of the core and is called a *drain.* Sand is used because water will pass through it easily. The sand allows the small amount of water that might seep through the core to run out the back of the dam.

Giant dump truck speeds up the work.

HAND COMPACTORS.

There must be a way of releasing water through the dam so there will be a supply of water downstream.

A large pipe called a *conduit* is run through the dam. The conduit pipe is carried to the dam in trucks and unloaded with a crane.

After the conduit is in place, dirt is packed tightly around the pipe with *hand compactors.*

Hand compactors pack the dirt down.

THE OUTLET

Later an *outlet* structure will be built on the upstream end of the conduit. The outlet looks something like the drain in a city street but it is much larger. Water will run into it and out through the conduit.

Bars of concrete are put over the open end of the outlet to keep trash from getting into the conduit.

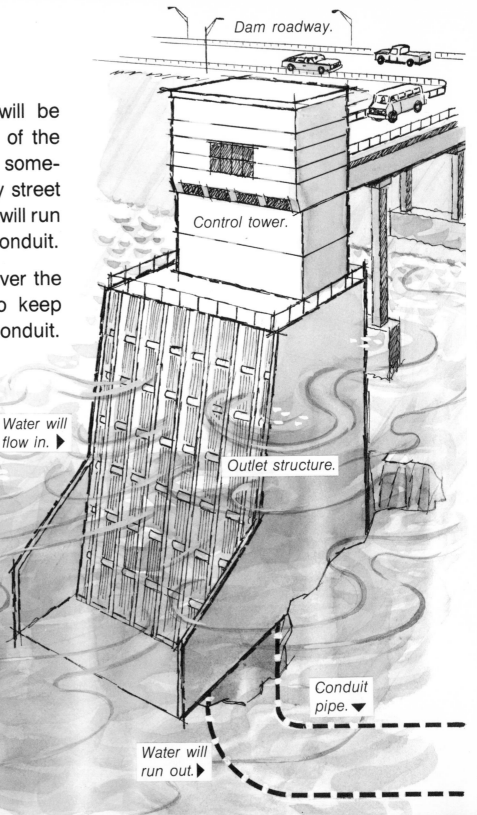

Dam roadway.

Control tower.

Water will flow in. ▶

Outlet structure.

Conduit pipe. ▼

Water will run out. ▶

Inside control tower.

THE CONTROL TOWER

A small building called a *control tower* is built on top of the outlet. A person in the control tower can push a lever and stop the water from going through the conduit. The outlet works much like the plug in a bathtub.

FINISHING THE EARTHFILL DAM

GRADER.

SCRAPER.

The bottom of the earthfill dam is much thicker than the top. When all of the dirt has been put in and packed down hard, it is just wide enough at the top for one scraper to unload at a time.

Motor graders are used to keep the surface of the dam very smooth.

Bottom of the dam is much wider than the top.

OFF-HIGHWAY TRUCKS.

RIPRAP

Grass will be planted on the downstream slope to keep the rain from washing the dirt away. But something else must be done to the upstream side to keep the dirt from being washed away by the waves splashing against it.

A thick cover called stone *riprap* is placed on the upstream slope to protect it.

Off-highway trucks loaded with big stones rumble along the top of the dam. They dump the riprap stones down on the upstream slope.

Some of the stones do not land in the right place. So they are picked up with *rock tongs* that are swung into place by a crane. The rock tongs work like the claw of a giant bird. The claw picks up the big stones and drops them in the right place.

THE SPILLWAY

If you have ever tried to stop water from running down a ditch by piling dirt in the ditch, you probably learned something very important about building a dam.

The water finally rises high enough to spill over the top of the dirt. When it does, it soon washes the dam away. The dam builders must make a place for the high water to spill over. This place is called a *spillway* and it is made of concrete so it will not wash away.

The spillway may have moveable gates that open to let the water out and close to keep it in.

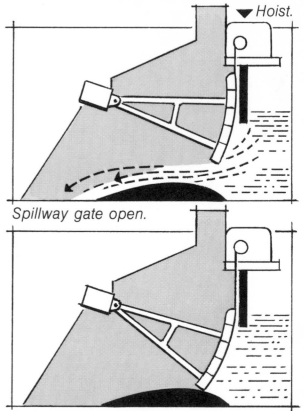

Spillway gate open.

Spillway gate closed.

Spillway.

The top of the dam must be higher than the spillway. This means that it will be higher than the water will ever go.

The part of the dam which sticks up above the water is called the *freeboard*. It is there to keep high waves from lapping over the top.

Freeboard.

Water Crest.

Most U.S. dams are earth and rockfill.

MASONRY DAMS

The most exciting dams of all are the masonry dams. These dams are usually made of stone or concrete and are very high but not as wide as earthfill dams.

Masonry dams are often built in places where it is hard to haul dirt. Often they are built in rocky and mountainous areas. Sometimes they are built in canyons where rock cliffs rise on either side.

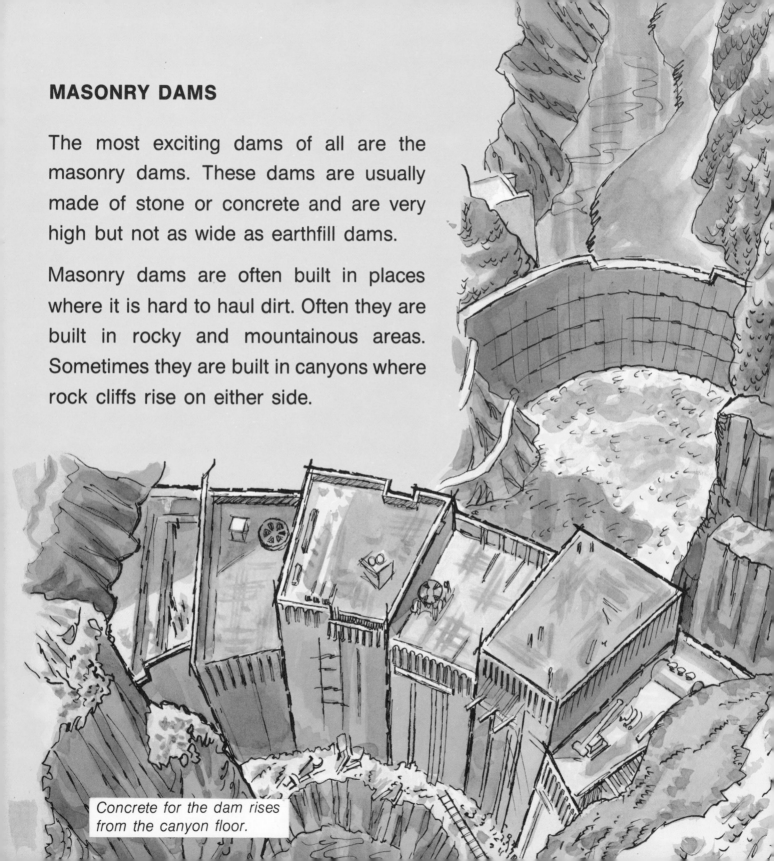

Concrete for the dam rises from the canyon floor.

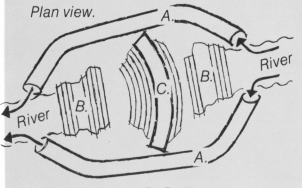

Plan view.

A. Diversion tunnels.
B. Cofferdams.
C. Dam.

DIVERSION TUNNELS

Just like the earthfill dam, coffer dams must be built first to make the water go around the dam site. This is hard to do, with big rock cliffs on both sides of the dam site.

Instead of a diversion ditch, *diversion tunnels* must be built. The tunnel is made through solid rock by first drilling small round holes about the size of a half dollar. The holes are made by *rock drills* which are mounted on a moving platform called a *jumbo.* A big jumbo may have several platforms with drills on it, one above the other.

Rock drills at work in tunnel.

BLASTING THE ROCK

DRILL, LOAD, EXPLODE.

When the holes have been driven in the rock, men push dynamite deep into the holes with long wooden poles. Then dirt is packed into the holes. When everything is ready, the men yell, "Fire in the hole!" Everybody knows that this means to move a safe distance away from the danger.

When everyone has left the tunnel, one man flips a lever that sends electricity through wires attached to the dynamite. The dynamite explodes with a loud boom and breaks up the rock into small pieces.

Men push dynamite deep into the holes.

FRONT-END WHEEL LOADERS LOAD OFF-HIGHWAY TRUCKS.

The broken-up rock is loaded into trucks by front-end loaders and hauled away. Some of the rock may be used to help make the coffer dams.

MAKING THE DAM SITE SAFE

As soon as the dam site is free of water, work can begin on the dam. Men are lowered from the top of the cliffs in *rope slings.* These slings look much like playground swings, but they are made to lower the men safely as they work.

The men use iron bars and small *jack hammers* to pry away loose rocks which might otherwise fall on the dam builders who will be working below later.

Rope slings hold men while they pry away loose rocks.

POWER SHOVEL.

OFF-HIGHWAY TRUCK.

POWER SHOVELS AND TRUCKS

Big, powerful *power shovels* are next moved into the dam site. A power shovel looks like a huge machine with a giant steel arm. On the end of the arm is a large steel box with steel teeth on the edge. Dirt and rocks are scooped up in the box and dumped into trucks.

These trucks are bigger than the trucks you see on the highway. They are called *off-highway trucks* because they are too big and heavy to drive on regular roads.

Off-highway trucks are loaded by big powerful shovels.

PREPARING THE FOUNDATIONS

The power shovel digs away the gravel and loose rock between the coffer dams. Finally it reaches a layer of rock called *bed rock*.

The bed rock has cracks in it which would let water escape under the dam. Holes are drilled into the bed rock. Then wet concrete is pumped into the holes. The wet concrete fills in all of the empty spaces in the rock and makes it watertight. This is called *grouting the foundation.*

Wet concrete (grout) is pumped into the holes.

Holes are drilled into the bedrock.

MIXING THE CONCRETE

Sand and gravel are fed into the concrete plant on *conveyors.* Conveyors are long belts that go 'round and 'round.

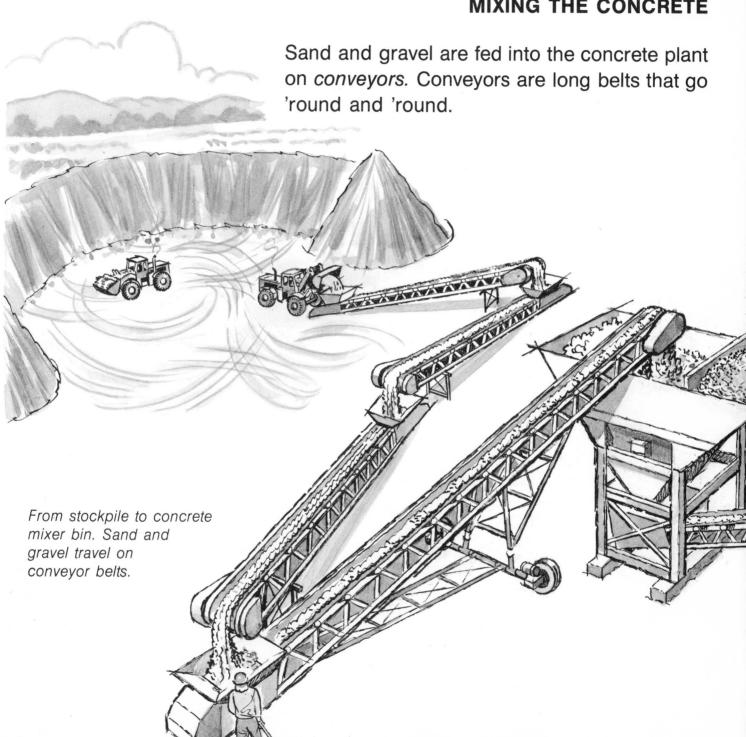

From stockpile to concrete mixer bin. Sand and gravel travel on conveyor belts.

THE CONCRETE PLANT

At last, everything is ready for the concrete. Special machines and many men will be used to mix the concrete and put it in the dam.

A concrete plant is assembled on the dam site.

The sand and gravel are mixed together with cement and water to make concrete. They are mixed in giant drums which look like those on concrete mixer trucks but are much larger.

Sand and gravel.

Water tank.

Cement.

Concrete plant.

HAULING THE CONCRETE IN BUCKETS

The concrete must be quickly moved to the dam after it is mixed. One way to do this is to take concrete to the dam in *concrete buckets*.

Filled concrete buckets are hauled to the dam on special trucks.

Concrete placing bucket.

Filled buckets are moved quickly to dam on special trucks.

HAULING THE CONCRETE IN BUCKETS

At the dam the concrete buckets are fastened onto the long wire ropes of big cranes. Then they are swung to the right place on the dam. Even though they are really very heavy, they look like big balloons floating through the air.

Small doors on the bottom of the concrete buckets can be opened by pulling a big lever on the side.

HAULING THE CONCRETE BY CABLEWAYS

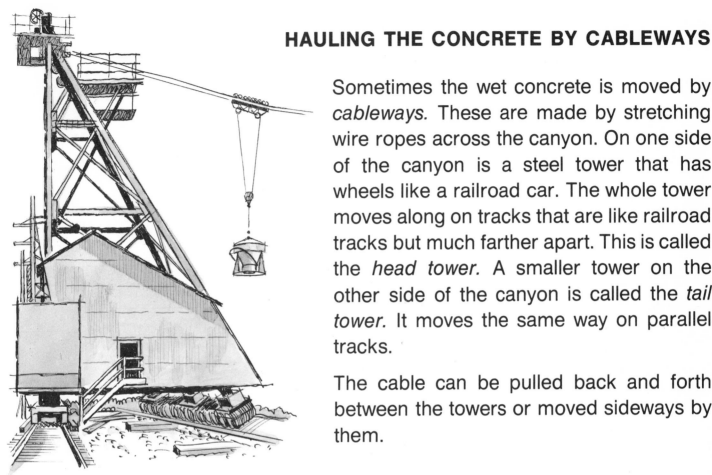

Cableway head tower.

Sometimes the wet concrete is moved by *cableways.* These are made by stretching wire ropes across the canyon. On one side of the canyon is a steel tower that has wheels like a railroad car. The whole tower moves along on tracks that are like railroad tracks but much farther apart. This is called the *head tower.* A smaller tower on the other side of the canyon is called the *tail tower.* It moves the same way on parallel tracks.

The cable can be pulled back and forth between the towers or moved sideways by them.

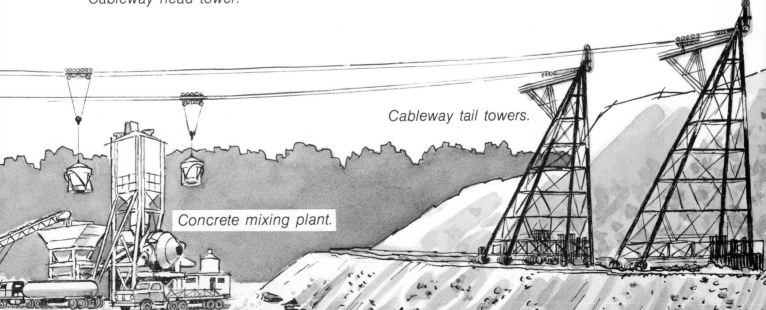

Cableway tail towers.

Concrete mixing plant.

HAULING THE CONCRETE BY CABLEWAYS

Attached to the big cable are smaller cables that hang straight down. On the end of these smaller cables is a concrete bucket which can be raised or lowered.

CONTROLLING THE CABLEWAYS

The man who operates the cableway sits at a *control panel* in the head tower. By pushing buttons and levers he can move the concrete buckets to any part of the dam.

Sometimes the place where he will dump the concrete is far away. So the man may watch where he puts the concrete on a closed-circuit television set.

He can also talk to the men on the dam with a two-way radio.

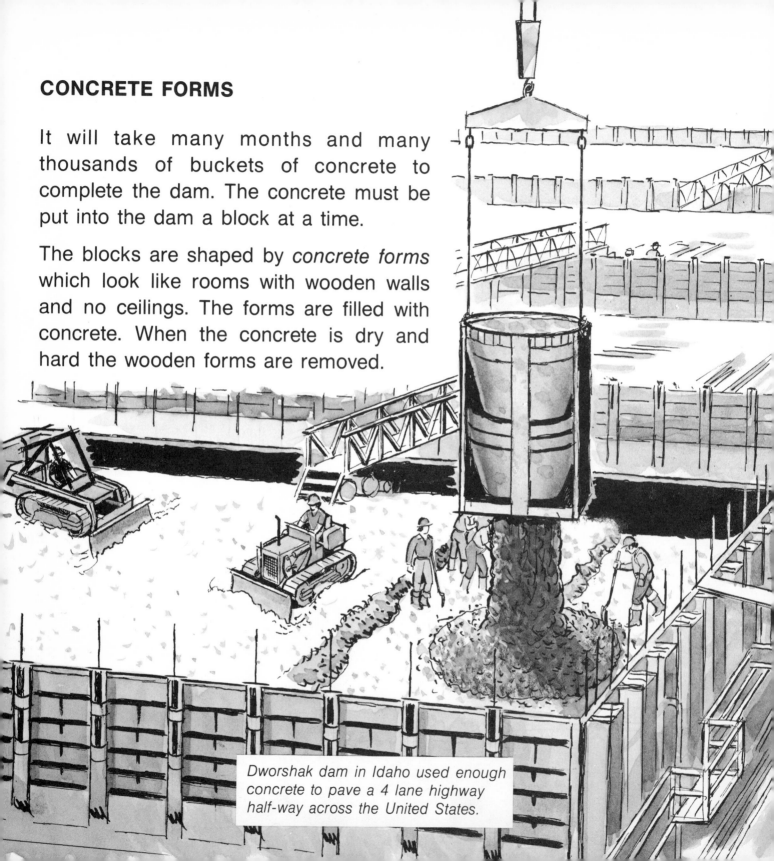

CONCRETE FORMS

It will take many months and many thousands of buckets of concrete to complete the dam. The concrete must be put into the dam a block at a time.

The blocks are shaped by *concrete forms* which look like rooms with wooden walls and no ceilings. The forms are filled with concrete. When the concrete is dry and hard the wooden forms are removed.

Dworshak dam in Idaho used enough concrete to pave a 4 lane highway half-way across the United States.

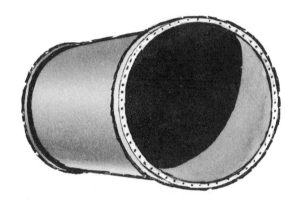

Collapsible wooden forms are used to make openings in the dam when concrete is poured around them.

PENSTOCKS

Concrete is poured over round wooden forms that are shaped like long tin cans. After the concrete has hardened, the forms are removed and big steel pipes called *penstocks* are put in the holes left in the concrete.

These penstocks will carry the water through the dam to the generators.

After forms are removed huge steel pipes are placed in the holes.

POURING THE CONCRETE

Day after day, month after month, the big concrete buckets dump the wet concrete into the dam.

Some dams are so big that it takes as many as three years just to pour the concrete in them!

Block after block of wet concrete is poured.

When a row of blocks goes clear across the width of the dam it is called a *lift*. Each lift makes the dam higher.

FILLING THE RESERVOIR

At last all of the concrete is in place and the last wooden forms are removed. The huge generators are moved into big rooms in the lower part of the dam.

When everything is ready, the gates on the diversion tunnels are closed. The dam then begins to do its job.

First, water begins to fill up the canyon behind the dam. Each time that it rains upstream, more water runs down into the reservoir.

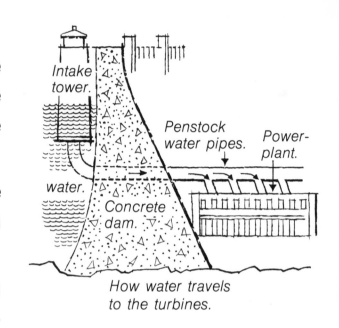

How water travels to the turbines.

Power plant interior showing generators.

Hoover Dam, one of the world's largest.

THE DAM, READY TO SERVE THE PEOPLE

It will be a long time before the reservoir is full. If the dam is big it may take several years to fill. When it is full there will be a great lake. People will swim and fish in the lake, and boats will sail on it.

Then the valves in the dam will be opened and water will pour through the penstock pipes. The rushing water will turn the turbines on great generators to make electricity. It will make life better and easier for the people. Some of the water will be sent through pipes to water the crops of farms near the dam.

The dam builders have done their job well.

Irrigation transforms desserts into farm land.

Recreational facilities become available.

Electric power is sent to
cities and rural areas.

Water is stored and
flow regulated.

Swimming, boating, water sports, camping
and outdoor activities can be developed.